Potential Environmental and Environmental-Health Implications of the SAFRR Tsunami Scenario in California

Open-File Report 2013–1170–F
California Geological Survey Special Report 229

U.S. Department of the Interior
U.S. Geological Survey

The SAFRR (Science Application for Risk Reduction) Tsunami Scenario

Stephanie Ross and Lucile Jones, Editors

Potential Environmental and Environmental-Health Implications of the SAFRR Tsunami Scenario in California

By Geoffrey S. Plumlee, Suzette A. Morman, and Carma San Juan

Open-File Report 2013–1170–F

California Geological Survey Special Publication 229

U.S. Department of the Interior
U.S. Geological Survey

U.S. Department of the Interior
SALLY JEWELL, Secretary

U.S. Geological Survey
Suzette M. Kimball, Acting Director

U.S. Geological Survey, Reston, Virginia 2013

For product and ordering information:
World Wide Web: http://www.usgs.gov/pubprod
Telephone: 1-888-ASK-USGS

For more information on the USGS—the Federal source for science about the Earth,
its natural and living resources, natural hazards, and the environment:
World Wide Web: http://www.usgs.gov
Telephone: 1-888-ASK-USGS

Suggested citation:
Plumlee, G.S., Morman, S.A., and San Juan, C., 2013, Potential Environmental and Environmental-Health Implications of the SAFRR Tsunami Scenario in California, chap. F, *in* Ross, S.L., and Jones, L.M., eds., The SAFRR (Science Application for Risk Reduction) Tsunami Scenario: U.S. Geological Survey Open-File Report 2013–1170, 34 p., http://pubs.usgs.gov/of/2013/1170/f/.

STATE OF CALIFORNIA
EDMUND G. BROWN JR.
GOVERNOR

THE NATURAL RESOURCES AGENCY
JOHN LAIRD
SECRETARY FOR RESOURCES

DEPARTMENT OF CONSERVATION
MARK NECHODOM
DIRECTOR

CALIFORNIA GEOLOGICAL SURVEY
JOHN G. PARRISH, Ph.D.
STATE GEOLOGIST

Contents

Potential Environmental and Environmental-Health Implications of the U.S. Geological Survey Science Application for Risk Reduction California Tsunami Scenario

By Geoffrey S. Plumlee, Suzette A. Morman, and Carma San Juan

Abstract

The California Tsunami Scenario models the impacts of a hypothetical, yet plausible, tsunami caused by an earthquake offshore from the Alaska Peninsula. In this chapter, we interpret plausible tsunami-related contamination, environmental impacts, potential for human exposures to contaminants and hazardous materials, and implications for remediation and recovery.

Inundation-related damages to major ports, boat yards, and many marinas could release complex debris, crude oil, various fuel types and other petroleum products, some liquid bulk cargo and dry bulk cargo, and diverse other pollutants into nearby coastal marine environments and onshore in the inundation zone. Tsunami-induced erosion of contaminated harbor bottom sediments could re-expose previously sequestered metal and organic pollutants (for example, organotin or DDT).

Inundation-related damage to many older buildings could produce debris containing lead paint, asbestos, pesticides, and other legacy contaminants. Intermingled household debris and externally derived debris and sediments would be left in flooded buildings. Post tsunami, mold would likely develop in inundated houses, buildings, and debris piles. Tsunamigenic fires in spilled oil, debris, cargo, vehicles, vegetation, and residential, commercial, or industrial buildings and their contents would produce potentially toxic gases and smoke, airborne ash, and residual ash/debris containing caustic alkali solids, metal toxicants, asbestos, and various organic toxicants. Inundation of and damage to wastewater treatment plants in many coastal cities could release raw sewage containing fecal solids, pathogens, and waste chemicals, as well as chemicals used to treat wastewaters.

Tsunami-related physical damages, debris, and contamination could have short- and longer-term impacts on the environment and the health of coastal marine and terrestrial ecosystems. Marine habitats in intertidal zones, marshes, sloughs, and lagoons could be damaged by erosion or sedimentation, and could receive an influx of debris, metal and organic contaminants, and sewage-related pathogens. Debris and re-exposed contaminated sediments would be a source of sea- or rain-water-leachable metal and organic contaminants that could pose chronic toxicity threats to ecosystems.

If human populations are successfully evacuated prior to the tsunami arrival, there would be no or limited numbers of drownings, other casualties, or related injuries, wounds, and infections. Immediately after the tsunami, human populations away from the inundation zone could be transiently exposed to airborne gases, smoke, and ash from tsunamigenic fires. Cleanup and disposal, particularly of hazardous materials, would pose substantial logistical challenges and economic costs. Given the high value of the coastal residential and commercial properties in the inundation zone, it can be postulated that there would be substantial insurance claims for environmental restoration, mold mitigation, disposal of debris that contains hazardous materials, and costs of litigation related to environmental liability.

Post-tsunami cleanup, if done with appropriate mitigation (for example, dust control), personal protection, and disposal measures, would help reduce the potential for cleanup-worker and resident exposures to toxicants and pathogens in harbor waters, debris, soils, ponded waters, and buildings. A number of other steps can be taken by governments, businesses, and residents to help reduce the environmental impacts of tsunamis and to recover more quickly from these environmental impacts. For example, development of State and local policies that foster rapid assessment of potential contamination, as well as rapid decision making for disposal options should hazardous debris or sediment be identified, would help enhance recovery by speeding cleanup.

Introduction

The tsunami scenario, developed by the U.S. Geological Survey (USGS) Science Applications for Risk Reduction (SAFRR) Project, models the generation, hydrology, and impacts on the California coast of a hypothetical yet plausible tsunami triggered by an earthquake in the subduction zone offshore of the Alaska Peninsula. A primary goal of this scenario is to help educate emergency planners, businesses, universities, government agencies, and other stakeholders about plausible effects of future tsunamis, so that they can be better prepared for and their impacts can be better mitigated.

In the scenario tsunami, seismologists designed a scientifically plausible earthquake event off the Alaska Peninsula. Using information generated by the seismologists for the earthquake, other experts in marine and coastal hydrology modeled the propagation of tsunami waves from the source area to the target region along the California coast, with high resolution modeling of inundation along the California coast and in selected harbors. Based on the inundation and current modeling, other experts provided input on plausible damages that would result from the scenario tsunami (Porter and others, 2013).

In this report, we interpret plausible tsunami-related environmental impacts and contamination, plausible human exposures to contamination and hazardous materials, implications for human health impacts, and implications for post-tsunami remediation and recovery. Our study integrates (1) information on environmental and health impacts of past tsunamis, (2) a qualitative analysis of plausible environmental impacts that would result from tsunami-related damages modeled by other scenario colleagues, and (3) a qualitative GIS-based analysis of areas likely to be inundated by either the scenario tsunami or any future tsunamis that reach the full extent of historical tsunami inundation zones mapped by the California Emergency Management Agency (Cal OES).

This analysis is similar to ones conducted for the ShakeOut earthquake and ARkStorm winter storm scenarios (Plumlee and others, 2012, 2013). Our results indicate that the inundation, resulting damages, and debris from scenario tsunami on the California coasts and ports could (1) cause adverse impacts on the environment as a direct result of the tsunami, (2) pose challenges for debris cleanup and environmental restoration following the tsunami, and (3) plausibly cause some exposures of local populations to chemical and pathogen contaminants.

Background

Tsunamis caused by submarine subduction zone earthquakes, coastal or submarine volcanic eruptions, or submarine landslides can cause massive damage to the natural and built environments in low-lying coastal areas. This can, in turn, lead to widespread environmental contamination and potential health impacts on affected ecosystems and exposed human populations. Damages and resulting environmental and health impacts are greatest when the tsunami source is close to the affected land areas, such as the damages caused in Indonesia and Thailand by the 2004 Indonesia earthquake and tsunami (Basnayake and others, 2005; Srinivas and Nakagawa, 2008), and the damages in Japan from the 2011 Tohoku earthquake and tsunami (Bird and Grossman, 2011; Shibata and others, 2012).

Due to their generally lower wave heights and energy, damages from distant sourced tsunamis (termed "teletsunamis") typically are less intense and spatially extensive than those produced by tsunamis from nearby sources, but nonetheless can cause substantial damages. Recent examples include the damages to several California ports from the 2010 Chilean earthquake and the 2011 Tohoku earthquake (Wilson and others, 2012, 2013a).

Tsunamis can cause contamination of nearshore marine and onshore coastal environments by introducing diverse debris, organic and inorganic chemicals, and pathogens. Examples include (1) remobilization of previously contaminated sediments from harbor bottoms (Wilson and others, 2012, 2013a); (2) release of contaminants or toxicant-bearing debris from damaged port facilities, berthed ships or small watercraft, and inundated coastal communities or industrial/commercial facilities (fig. 1; Ratnapradipa and others, 2012; Shibata and others, 2012; Australian Broadcasting Corporation, 2013); (3) tsunami-triggered fires (Yamada and others, 2011); and (4) sewage releases from damaged wastewater-treatment infrastructure (Bird and Grossman, 2011; Tanabe and Subramanian, 2011; Shibata and others, 2012). Shallow aquifers in the areas of tsunami inundation can be contaminated by seawater, and transient salinization of agricultural fields and die offs of terrestrial vegetation because of saltwater poisoning have been noted in tsunami inundation areas (fig. 1; United Nations Environment Program, 2007; Yoshii and others, 2012; Chagué-Goff and others, 2012). The types and amounts of environmental contamination will vary according to the source.

The recent earthquake-driven tsunamis in Indonesia and Japan underscore the types of direct impacts on public health that major tsunamis can cause (Keim, 2011). In addition to large numbers of drownings, large tsunamis can cause various other health impacts that are uncommon in other types of disasters. These include fatalities, trauma, penetrating injuries, and wounds resulting from tsunami-borne debris, and the post-disaster development of wound infections and tetanus cases. Another unusual impact is the development of tsunami lung in large numbers of people who nearly drown in tsunami floodwaters. Tsunami lung is a necrotizing lung infection caused by pathogens commonly associated with seawater aspiration, and possibly other uncommon pathogens not associated with seawater (Keim, 2011). Tsunami-triggered fires also could result in fatalities.

Figure 1. Photograph of the damages caused by the massive tsunami generated by the March 2011 Tohoku earthquake that devastated the northeastern coast of Japan, taken in May 2011 in the Sanriku area. Few buildings were left standing, and extensive debris deposits were left behind. Also note the dying trees at the base of the hills in the background, which were closest to the tsunami inundation area—these were presumably suffering the effects of salt water poisoning. The California scenario tsunami would not cause nearly as extensive or complete devastation as seen in Japan, but would likely cause some damage to buildings in the inundated areas, and leave behind debris. Photograph by Bruce Jaffe, U.S. Geological Survey.

In the days and months following a tsunami, additional health impacts can develop. As with other types of natural disasters, outbreaks of infectious diseases, such as cholera, most commonly occur in overcrowded refugee camps where refugees lack access to adequate medical care and cannot practice good hygiene. Lack of accessible medical care also can exacerbate preexisting medical conditions. Another substantial concern is the development of psychosocial illnesses, such as post-traumatic stress disorder. As with other flood-related disasters, post-tsunami mold development may be a substantial health concern for people cleaning up and reoccupying flooded buildings (Manuel, 2013). Particularly in developed countries, loss of electrical power commonly results in the widespread use of gas-powered generators, which can, in turn, increase the potential for carbon monoxide poisoning.

The number of people who suffer direct health impacts from tsunamis is strongly influenced by many factors, including the type of the triggering event, proximity to tsunami source, offshore and onshore coastal topography, prevailing currents, tidal stage at the time of impact, population magnitudes in inundated areas, presence or absence of wave mitigation seawalls, building practices in the inundated areas, and the effectiveness of advance tsunami warnings and evacuation efforts prior to tsunami arrival. For example, the 2004 Indian Ocean tsunami triggered by the earthquake in Sumatra caused more than 225,000 deaths (U.S. Geological Survey, 2013) in nearby coastal areas, and tens of thousands of deaths in coastal Sri Lanka (900 mi away) and coastal India (more than 1,200 mi away). The tsunami triggered by the 2011 Japan Tohoku earthquake resulted in more than 15,000 fatalities in nearby coastal areas (National Oceanic and Atmospheric Administration, 2013). The 1946 Aleutian Island teletsunami (which occurred prior to the implementation of the Pacific Ocean tsunami warning system) killed more than 150 people in Hawaii. In contrast, teletsunamis from the 2010 Chile earthquake and the 2011 Japan Tohoku earthquake combined caused zero deaths and one death, respectively, when they hit the western coast of the United States.

Although a number of studies have summarized environmental impacts from recent tsunamis, health impacts that resulted from exposures to environmental contaminants (other than the pathogen-related infections noted previously) generally have not been identified or described in detail. This may be because (1) there have been relatively few modern tsunamis with extensive environmental impacts, (2) the heaviest exposures are transient, (3) contamination-related health impacts are small in magnitude compared to the much more visible direct health impacts, (4) it may take years after the disaster for adverse health impacts to develop, and (or) (5) adverse health impacts that are discovered may not be conclusively linked to tsunami-related environmental contamination causes.

Overview of the Approach

Based on the locations, types, and nature of the plausible damages to ports, harbors, marinas, and built areas described by Porter and others (2013) and other chapters in this full report, coupled with information on environmental impacts from past tsunamis, we inferred likely environmental consequences and potential for human exposures to scenario tsunami-triggered damages, debris, and contamination. We used Geographic Information Systems (GIS) analysis software ARC GIS to understand coastal areas where tsunami inundation could affect various potential sources of contamination. For the extent of inundation, we considered the plausible extent of inundation modeled by the tsunami scenario and the Cal OES zone of maximum inundation (Wilson and others, 2008, Barberopoulou and others, 2009), which was mapped based on the extent of flooding from all maximum considered, local and distant tsunami sources (fig. 2). The Cal OES inundation zone extends farther inland than the predicted SAFRR scenario inundation zone except for a few places; because of the higher resolution modeling, the SAFRR scenario shows inundation traveling further up some rivers and further onshore in areas of sudden topographic change. Examining both inundation zones allowed us to consider the scenario impacts and potential impacts from more extensive tsunamis similar to some that have occurred in the past. Where available, we also incorporated information on tsunami currents and wave height modeled by the scenario. This was particularly useful, for example, to evaluate where in the Ports of Los Angeles and Long Beach high currents could lead to substantial redistribution of contaminated harbor bottom sediments.

Using ARC GIS, we digitally overlaid tsunami inundation extent and depth maps on satellite/geography coverages to determine locations and sizes of both potential sources of contamination in the inundation zone and important features that could be adversely affected by inundation or tsunami-related contamination. Examples include: (1) harbors, marinas, and boat yards; (2) residential, commercial, or industrial areas; agricultural fields; (3) facilities such as oil refineries, power plants and wastewater treatment plants; and (4) lagoons, sloughs, or estuaries. The U.S. Environmental Protection Agency (EPA) Facilities Registry System database (U.S.

5

Environmental Protection Agency Facilities Registry System, 2011) was used to further identify and locate environmentally significant facilities (for example, wastewater-treatment plants, oil refineries, chemical manufacturing plants, gas stations, hospitals, schools) that would occur within or near the scenario or State inundation zones (fig. 3). State GIS coverages were used to identify critical species habitats in nearshore marine areas that could be affected by the tsunami (fig. 2). The mapping feature of various commercial web sites, which list county or municipal assessors data on individual mapped properties, were used to understand general ranges in age and value of residences located within the scenario and State inundation zones. Knowing the age of a building provides key insights into the potential contaminants that could be released: for example, buildings older than the late 1970s to early 1980s have a greater likelihood of containing legacy building materials, such as asbestos and lead-based paint, and legacy pesticides (Plumlee and others, 2012).

The general types of contamination that can be released from various potential sources in the inundation zone are relatively well understood (Plumlee and others, 2013). Once the potential sources and their plausible types of environmental contaminants were identified, we applied a general knowledge of contaminant transport, fate, and impacts to develop a qualitative understanding of how tsunami-related environmental damages and contamination might vary along the California coast. We then evaluated plausible contaminant exposure pathways to human populations.

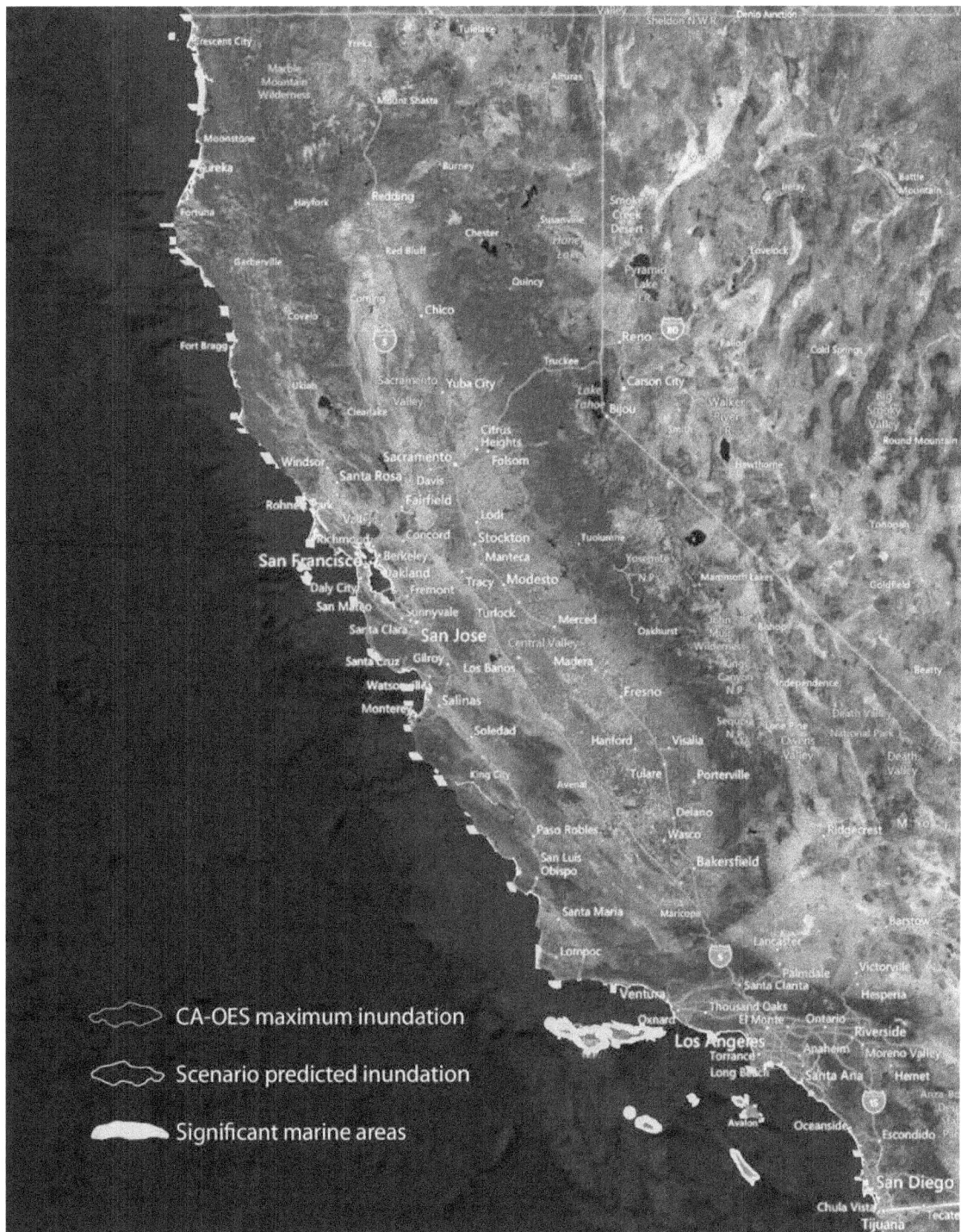

Figure 2. Map showing extent of the scenario predicted inundation zone and, where the coverage is more extensive, the California Emergency Management Agency (Cal OES) maximum tsunami inundation zone (Wilson and others, 2008; Barberopoulou and others, 2009). Significant marine areas (Areas of Special Biological Significance, State Marine Life Refuges, and State Marine Protected Areas) are also shown.

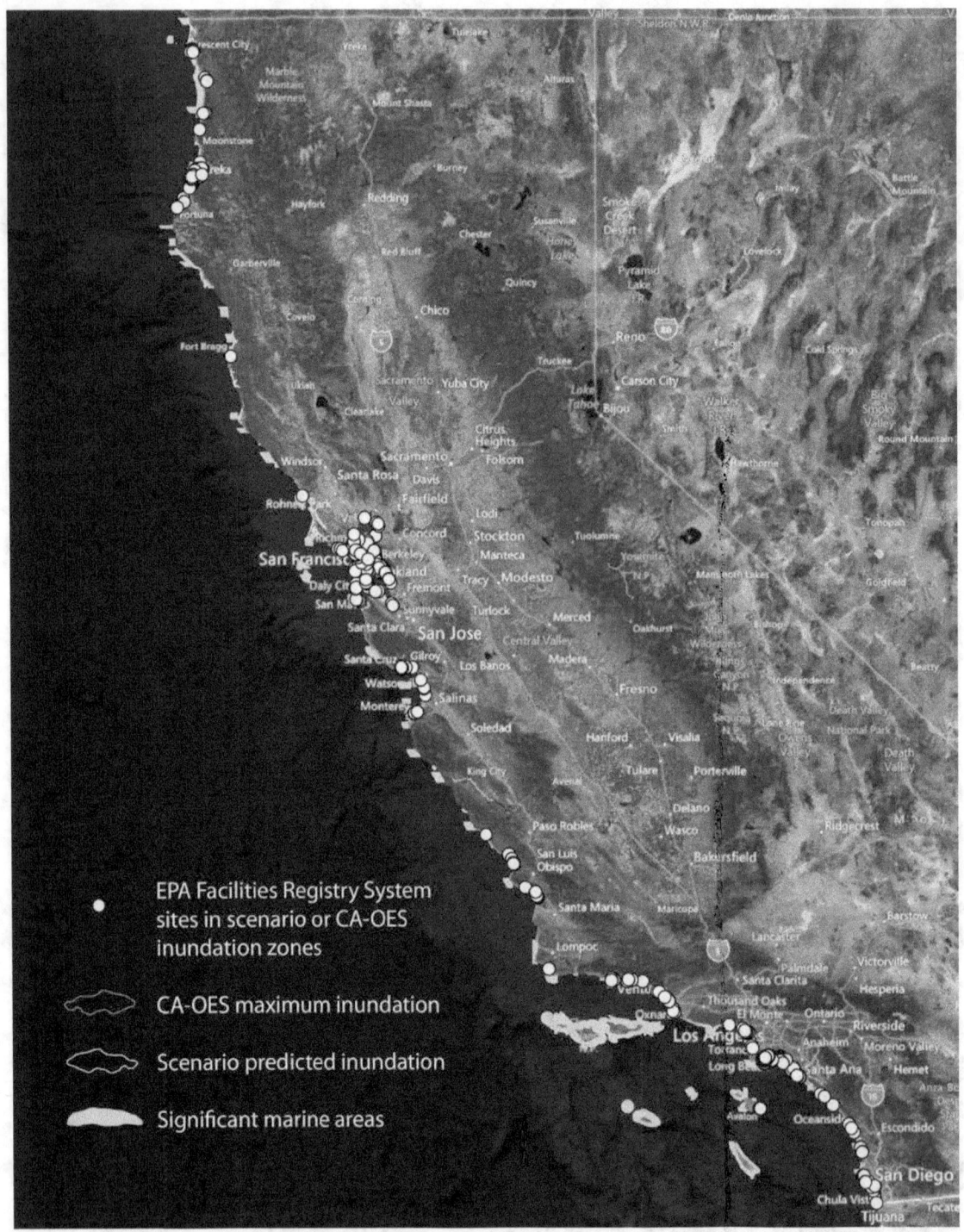

Figure 3. Map showing locations of environmentally significant facilities from the U.S. Environmental Protection Agency Facilities Registry System database (U.S. Environmental Protection Agency Facilities Registry System, 2011) indicated to fall within the predicted scenario inundation zone or the California Emergency Management Agency (Cal OES) maximum tsunami inundation zone.

Limitations of This Analysis

As noted by other chapters in this volume, there are uncertainties in the results of the modeled scenario tsunami inundation results. There also are uncertainties in the databases and other information available for our environmental analysis. Examples of these uncertainties include (1) incorrect locations or other incorrect information on environmentally significant facilities; (2) lack of detailed knowledge of potential cargos transported through ports that could be released as a result of tsunami damages; (3) lack of detailed information on the specific contaminants that are present in buildings, commercial facilities, or industrial facilities; (4) lack of information on the vulnerability of specific facilities, warehouses, or buildings to tsunami impacts and damages; and (5) lack of information on the magnitude of possible contaminant releases that could result from specific sources if they were to be damaged. As a result, this approach should only be considered as the first of multiple steps toward a more quantitative, predictive approach to understanding the potential sources, types, environmental behavior, and environmental and health implications of contaminants that could be released into the environment by coastal tsunamis.

Potential Contamination from Inundation of and Damage to Ports, Naval Yards, Harbors, and Marinas

Both the scenario and State inundation zones extend well into major coastal ports (San Diego, Los Angeles, Long Beach, Hueneme, San Francisco, Redwood City, Oakland, Richmond, Benicia, Humboldt Bay), major active or former naval yards or ports (San Diego, San Francisco, Vallejo), and harbors (for example, Huntington Beach, Newport Bay, Crescent City). Marinas in nearly every coastal city and town are also in both inundation zones.

Review of Damages to Ports

Porter and others (2013) detail the potential damages that the scenario tsunami could cause to the Ports of Los Angeles and Long Beach (fig. 4), and provide general overviews of potential damages to other ports (San Diego, San Francisco, Oakland, Richmond, and Humboldt Bay), several harbors, and a number of coastal marinas. Plausible impacts they identified at the Port of Long Beach (POLB) included:
- Inundation of specific dock areas and structures, such as administration buildings;
- Damages to docks, piers, and pilings;
- Some damages to containerized cargo and to dry bulk cargo (gypsum, petroleum coke, prilled sulfur, salt), but no damages to liquid bulk cargo;
- Damage to 2000 import vehicles, forklifts, dryage trucks, and other vehicles parked on docks; and
- Possible unmooring of large cargo vessel or tanker, but without release of oil.

Plausible impacts identified by Porter and others (2013) at Port of Los Angeles (POLA) include
- Inundation of specific dock areas;
- Limited damages to containerized cargo;
- Some damages to dry bulk cargo (industrial borates);
- No damages to bulk cargo;
- Damages to about 650 import cars on the docks;

· Sinking of and(or) extensive damages to thousands of small watercraft, as well as damages to facilities at 16 port marinas.

The scenario model predicted sufficiently high currents in some parts of both POLA and POLB to result in significant sediment scour and redeposition.

Figure 4. Satellite image of the Ports of Los Angeles and Long Beach, with map overlays showing: (a) boundaries of the scenario (cyan) and California Emergency Management Agency (Cal OES) maximum (magenta) inundation zones; (b) U.S. Environmental Protection Agency (EPA) Facilities Registry System sites (yellow dots, U.S. Environmental Protection Agency Facilities Registry System, 2011) within the inundation zones; (c) DDT concentrations (blue dots) exceeding 16 nanograms per gram (8 times the numeric target concentration) in samples of harbor sediments collected and analyzed by Weston (2009a,b); and (d) open yellow circles showing areas of highest current velocity predicted for the scenario tsunami by Lynett and Son *in* The SAFRR Tsunami Modeling Working Group (2013).

The Port of San Diego was predicted by the scenario to not experience inundation of its two marine terminals, but a large number of Navy piers were predicted to be inundated (Porter and others, 2013). Many different marinas within San Diego Bay and Mission Bay to the north were predicted to sustain significant damages as part of the scenario tsunami.

At Port Hueneme, some docks and warehouses were predicted to be inundated by the scenario tsunami, but the automobile import terminal was not. Significant sediment scour also was predicted to occur.

At San Francisco, a number of the piers, including Port Hueneme headquarters, substantial amounts of commercial real estate (particularly pier 39 and Fisherman's Wharf), and piers that receive predominantly break bulk cargo (such as steel, lumber, and other large objects) were predicted to be in the scenario inundation zone (Porter and others, 2013). Substantial damage to the commercial fishing fleet, docks, and a fish processing facility also was deemed plausible.

At the ports of Oakland, Richmond, and Redwood City, a number of docks, piers, container yards, bulk cargo areas, and some import auto offloading areas were expected to be inundated by the scenario tsunami. Multiple small craft marinas around San Francisco Bay also were likely to be inundated and damaged. A high concentration of oil storage tanks was noted in the scenario inundation zone at the port of Richmond (Porter and others, 2013; Scawthorne, 2013).

Scawthorn (2013) and Porter and others (2013) identified 17 large petroleum facilities (mostly tank farms) along the California coast (see example in fig. 5) where inundation-related damage (such as floating of large oil tanks from their foundations or breakage of piping) could potentially cause significant releases of flammable petroleum liquids that would float on the water surface. The scenario model indicates that artificial islands hosting oil-drilling platforms adjacent to the Port of Long Beach (White, Grim, Chaffee, Freeman) could plausibly be inundated (R. Wilson, Cal OES, written comm., 2013). This could lead to possible oil releases from damage to oil tanks and piping. Damage to gasoline storage tanks and transfer piping at many marinas could plausibly result in the release of smaller quantities of flammable gasoline. If ignited (most plausibly by electrical sparks), oil or gasoline releases could turn into waterborne fires that could then engulf wood piers, ships, and small watercraft, as well as buildings, vehicles, cargo, and vegetation in the inundation zone. Porter and others (2013) and Scawthorne (2013) identified a number of measures implemented at many California ports that have helped mitigate or prevent oil releases; these include installing oil storage tanks within secondary containment units, and installing rapid valve turnoffs that restrict oil flow through vulnerable piping when a potentially damaging tsunami, earthquake or other disaster is anticipated.

Our analysis indicates that the scenario tsunami and any tsunami reaching the full extent of the Cal OES inundation zone in the various ports, harbors, and marinas could release a variety of debris and potential contaminants into the marine environment and the onshore inundation zone. Depending on the materials released and the processes by which the releases occur, these materials could (1) become airborne as gases or particulate matter; contaminate onshore soils, beaches, paved surfaces, or inundated buildings; (2) contaminate harbor bottoms and nearshore marine sediments; (3) form immiscible liquid plumes that float or sink in seawater; (4) have contaminants that leach into seawater or rainfall; and (or) (5) have materials that could either coat or be ingested directly by terrestrial or marine organisms.

11

Figure 5. This satellite image shows port facilities, including a marine oil terminal, indicated to lie partially within the scenario tsunami inundation zone (transparent blue-green). The entire area of the image lies within the California Emergency Management Agency (Cal OES) maximum inundation zone.

Debris

Physical damages to piers, buildings, large and small watercraft, import automobiles parked on docks, drayage trucks, and other vehicles on docks could produce substantial quantities of debris containing a wide range of organic, metal, and other contaminants. A few examples include:

- Ammoniacal copper zinc arsenate (ACZA)-, chrome-copper-arsenate (CCA)- or creosote-treated wood from pier pilings and wood docks;
- Asbestos-containing insulation or lead paint released into the waters, air, and dock areas from damaged older facilities;
- Materials found in or used to construct ships and small watercraft of varying ages (for example, antifouling paints with copper or other metals; fiberglass; plastics; asbestos insulation; Styrofoam; rope; fishing nets; motor parts; electronics; batteries; lead ship ballast); and
- Various debris types such as automobile glass, concrete dusts and debris, mercury from fluorescent lights or older thermostats in buildings, and containers of paints and other chemicals.

It is not clear whether damage to large cargo containers would be sufficient to cause releases of their contents, but if so, then a potentially wide range of container cargo could also be released.

The debris could either be deposited on land or remain in the ocean. Heavier debris would sink to the harbor bottoms, but many of the debris types noted above would float and could be carried by currents to coastal areas outside the ports.

Debris will pose a range of potential environmental hazards. Rainwater and seawater can leach a variety of inorganic and organic toxicants. For example, hexavalent chromium, copper, zinc, and arsenic are readily leached from AZCA-treated wood, and polycyclic aromatic hydrocarbons (PAHs) are readily leached from creosote-treated wood by both rain water and sea water (Stratus, 2006a, 2006b). This leaching could be accelerated by tsunami-induced wood breakage that exposures fresh wood surfaces for leaching. Metals, such as copper and organotin, could be leached from watercraft debris. Seawater corrosion could release a wide range of metals from steel, electronics, wiring, and other debris. As shown by the Tohoku tsunami, many types of floating debris are combustible, and so can be ignited (most likely by burning petroleum products) and burn. Accelerated oxidation of iron metal in debris piles by seawater salts also can trigger spontaneous ignition (Sekizawa and Sasaki, 2011). Freshly broken concrete can react with water to produce transient, locally significant caustic alkalinity in any waters it encounters; this alkalinity would likely diminish substantially over time. Small debris could become available for ingestion by animals or fish, and land and sea animals could become entangled in debris, such as ropes or fishing nets.

Potential Releases of Petroleum or Petroleum Products

Porter and others (2013) concluded that there would likely not be releases of petroleum liquid bulk cargo from the Ports of Los Angeles and Long Beach, nor would there be sufficient damage to the predicted one unmoored major vessel to produce an oil spill. Nonetheless, the number of potential sources for crude oil or petroleum products in the scenario and State inundation zones raises the likelihood that tsunamis could trigger multiple spills in California ports, Navy yards, harbors, and marinas having a range of sizes and compositions. These spills could come from tsunami-damaged marine oil terminals (fig. 5), refineries, small watercraft, chemical facilities, automobiles, dryage trucks, and other vehicles or equipment in the zone of inundation. Bulk petroleum cargo types that could be released in potentially large volumes include unrefined crude oil and various types of jet, bunker, and diesel fuel. Damage to fuel tanks in watercraft or vehicles would release small volumes of various vehicle-dependent fuel types.

The environmental behavior of oil and petroleum spills is well known. The more toxic fuel components (benzene, toluene, ethylbenzene, and xylenes) primarily volatilize following spills, which could create a potential inhalation exposure for cleanup workers, other people, and terrestrial organisms in the area. There also could be some dissolution of these components into seawater, with possible impacts on aquatic organisms that contact the affected seawater. Less toxic but stable heavier petroleum components would form emulsions by wave action and slowly degrade over time through photodegradation and biodegradation. Eventually, the heaviest, most tar-rich fractions could be deposited on beaches or settle to the bottom of harbors or nearshore marine environments, where they would cement bottom sediments.

Spill remediation approaches include skimming, intentional burning, and (or) application of chemical dispersants. Burning produces large amounts of smoke and leaves behind some residual oil ash material that can be enriched in the metals found in oils, most commonly nickel and vanadium. The application of dispersants is intended to promote dispersion of oil into smaller droplets that are more readily sorbed onto fine sediment particles that settle out.

A number of natural oil seeps from the sea floor are present along the southern California coast. These result in a natural baseline contribution of oil to the marine environment, and the baseline accumulation of tar and oil residues on local beaches (U.S. Geological Survey Seeps, 2013).

A broad range of impacts has been noted on organisms that contact spilled oil, petroleum products, or chemical dispersants applied to help disperse spilled oil. These can include (National Oceanic and Atmospheric Administration Fisheries Service, 2013):

· Oiling of bird feathers, which would inhibit flight and disrupt temperature regulation;
· Oiling of sea mammal fur, which would inhibit temperature regulation;
· Inhalation of vapors, which could lead to irritation of the respiratory tract; ingestion, which could cause injuries to the gastrointestinal tract and affect the animals' ability to digest or absorb foods;
· Dermal contact, which could cause skin irritation, chemical burns, and infections;
· Toxicity effects from absorption, such as liver, kidney, and brain damage;
· Chronic effects such as decreased reproductive success; and
· Dermal contact with and ingestion of water containing dissolved oil components.

Potential Releases of Liquid Cargo

Porter and others (2013) concluded that, based on locations of the specific piers predicted to be or not be inundated, no liquid cargo would be released as a result of the tsunami in the ports of Los Angeles, Long Beach, or San Diego, but it is unclear whether that is the case for other ports. As a result, some discussion is warranted here as to the types of liquid cargo that pass through the ports, and potential environmental concerns if there were to be tsunami-related releases of these liquid cargos.

In addition to the cargo types identified by Porter and others (2013) to pass through POLA and POLB, information on liquid cargo types passing through other California ports can be gleaned from their web sites. Cedre (2013) provided a general overview of liquid and solid bulk cargo types that have been associated with releases around the world, as well as an overview of their potential environmental impacts. In addition to crude oil and petroleum products, examples of other liquid bulk cargo types in transit through California ports (and possibly manufactured at the ports) that have been noted include liquid chemicals (for example, fertilizers and ethanol), milk, juice, and vegetable oils. The environmental behavior of a released cargo will depend on characteristics, such as how it interacts with seawater (for example, its solubility or immiscibility), and the volatility of its components. Although many of these liquid cargo materials are not toxic, large volume releases of some types can still have adverse environmental impacts. For example, vegetable oils can cause oiling of birds' feathers, asphyxiate benthic fauna, form polymers that cement beach sands and sediments, and generate noxious odors as they are biodegraded (Cedre, 2004).

Potential Releases of Dry Bulk Cargo

The scenario indicated that several types of dry bulk cargo would be affected by inundation at POLA and POLB, including industrial borates, gypsum, prilled sulfur (small pellets of elemental sulfur), and petroleum coke (Weston, 2009a, 2009b; Porter and others,

2013). A variety of other dry bulk cargo types have been indicated to pass through various California ports, such as cement, coal, salt, metallurgical coke, solid fertilizers, sand, gravel, aggregate, rice, cottonseed, and bauxite (Tioga, 2002; Porter and others, 2013).

If dry cargo storage facilities are damaged by the tsunami, then there could be some potential for dispersal of the cargo into the environment. Tsunami waters could redistribute the cargoes within the inundation zone, or carry them into the marine environment. Damages to containment structures could expose remaining cargo to wind dispersion, rainfall, and rainfall-induced runoff.

Different dry cargo types will have substantial differences in their environmental behavior if they are released. For example, cement can react initially with rainwater or seawater to produce runoff containing caustic alkalinity; however, the alkalinity in runoff would diminish over time as the caustic solids in the cement are neutralized by carbonic acid in the rainwater. Depending on the cement type, various metals, such as hexavalent chromium and zinc, could be leached from the cement into the waters. Prilled sulfur could react over time with rainfall to produce sulfuric acid-rich runoff. Further, prilled sulfur is an easily ignitable, combustible solid that will produce sulfur dioxide and other toxic sulfur oxide gases when burned. Petroleum coke, a carbon- and ash-rich solid produced as a residual of refining processes, can, depending on the source oil composition, contain low to high levels of sulfur, nickel, vanadium, iron, and other metals or metalloids that may be leachable into water. Its dusts can become flammable and explosive. Prilled sulfur and petroleum coke dusts, if inhaled, could result in respiratory tract irritation.

Further work is needed to understand whether these dry cargos would be released, and if so, released in sufficient quantities for these impacts to be substantial in more than just the areas immediately adjacent to cargo handling and storage facilities.

Potential Impacts from Inundated Shipbuilding and Boat Repair Yards

A substantial number of active and closed shipbuilding and boat repair yards (which we will refer to as boatyards) occur within the scenario and (or) Cal OES inundation zones. Boatyards have been identified as the one of the many potential sources for metal and organic contaminants in POLA and POLB harbor sediments, such as copper, zinc, lead, organotin, polychlorinated biphenyls, and polycyclic aromatic hydrocarbons (Weston, 2009a, 2009b). A 2006 study found that Puget Sound boatyards could be a substantial source of lubrication oil, copper, zinc, lead, various organotin forms, PAHs, phenols, methylphenols, and phthalates in stormwater runoff into harbors (Johnson and others, 2006).

These contaminants were used in topside paints, antifouling hull paints, paint removal, oil-based products used as fuels or in engine or equipment lubrication (Johnson and others, 2006; Weston 2009a, 2009b). Zinc also is sourced from sacrificial metals used to protect propellers, shafts, and other metal parts. In addition to its past use in legacy paints, lead is still used in ballast keels. Phthalates are used in plasticizers and adhesives.

Both copper and organotin were designed to leach from antifouling hull paints, so that the paints would be toxic to barnacles or other marine organisms trying to grow on the hulls. As a result, antifouling paints also can be a source of seawater contamination. Organotin was used extensively in antifouling bottom paints prior to the mid-2000s, but its use has been banned in the United States since 2008 due to its adverse environmental impacts. Copper is still in use as a component of antifouling paints, although various port jurisdictions are investigating ways to diminish its usage and resulting impacts.

As described for POLA and POLB (Water Resources Action Plan, 2009; Weston, 2009a, 2009b), a number of ports and boatyards are implementing measures to reduce runoff and other contamination into harbors. However, it is plausible that some inundated boatyards could serve as sources of contaminant-bearing debris (for example, lead from ballast manufacture, hull pieces, insulation, others) and water-borne dissolved or suspended particulate contaminants in the tsunami waters. Some of these contaminants, such as organotin or organotin-bearing woods, would be legacies from past practices at the boatyards.

Scour and Redistribution of Contaminated Harbor Sediments

The 2010 Chilean and 2011 Tohoku tsunamis triggered extensive scour and redistribution of sediments in the Crescent City and Santa Cruz Harbors (Wilson and others, 2012, 2013a). It is likely that the stronger and more spatially damaging scenario tsunami would lead to similar issues in a number of coastal harbors.

A review of the literature indicates that contaminated harbor bottom sediments are a substantial concern at many California ports (for example, see Water Resources Action Plan, 2009 and Weston 2009a, 2009b, for discussions about the Ports of Los Angeles and Long Beach) (fig. 4). The contamination includes a variety of metals (for example, lead, zinc, copper, arsenic, mercury, nickel, vanadium, organotin), metal sulfides (in anoxic sediments), many different organic chemicals (crude oil components, PAHs, PCBs, DDT and other pesticides, phthalates, and others), and diverse debris. There are many different sources to which this contamination has been attributed, and has resulted through intentional practices, accidental releases, or (in some areas) natural processes. Examples of potential sources include (for example, van Geen and Luoma, 1999; Water Resources Action Plan, 2009):

· Shipbuilding or boat repair yards;
· Spills from petroleum storage, transfer, or refinery facilities;
· Releases from ships or smaller watercraft;
· Releases from cargo storage or handling facilities;
· Releases from pesticide or other chemical manufacturing plants;
· Wastes from manufacturing or fabricating activities;
· Military bases;
· Wastewater-treatment plants;
· Fish-processing plants;
· Stormwater runoff inputs from docks, industrial areas, and major highways adjacent to the ports;
· Inputs of contaminated waters and sediments from rivers at some ports;
· In the Bay area, contamination from upstream historical mining operations (for example, mercury mining and mercury amalgamation gold extraction in the Coast Ranges and Sierra Nevada foothills);
· Atmospheric deposition;
· Sediments from outside the harbors carried into the harbors by marine currents; and
· Natural oil seeps.

The ports are actively pursuing policies and practices to minimize ongoing contamination. Examples include (for example, Water Resources Action Plan, 2009):
· Working with port tenants and nearby municipal entities to implement practices that reduce contamination;

16

· Implementing better practices to manage storm waters and fugitive dust emissions from port facilities;
· Working with marinas to minimize discharges from small watercraft and reduce other potential sources of contamination;
· Improving port trash collection programs; and
· Enhancing sustainability programs in port facilities.

A variety of activities have been undertaken, are ongoing, or are planned to locate and remediate the most heavily contaminated sediment accumulations in key parts of many harbors. Examples of remediation methods used include: (1) dredging of contaminated sediments, with onland storage of the removed sediments in secured disposal areas, and (2) capping of contaminated underwater sediment deposits with uncontaminated sediments.

Tsunami-triggered sediment erosion and redistribution (fig. 4) could undo remediation efforts by re-depositing contaminated sediments in previously remediated parts of harbors, or by re-exposing capped sediment deposits. It also could complicate ongoing remediation efforts by commingling contaminated sediments with sunken debris, diluting contaminants by commingling contaminated sediments with uncontaminated sediments, or altering the previously mapped distribution of contaminated sediments in need of remediation.

Resuspension of sediments from the harbor bottoms into the water column would enhance their exposure to aquatic organisms, which could directly ingest the sediment particles. Sediment resuspension also would likely result in chemical transformations, such as oxidation (for example, of metal sulfides, metal(loid)s of variable oxidation state, such as arsenic), desorption of contaminants from particles, and volatilization of volatile components brought to the water-atmosphere interface. Past tsunamis also have transported marine sediments onto land in the inundation zone. Any contaminated sediment deposits left behind in the inundation zone also could undergo a variety of transformations, such as sulfide oxidation (and resulting formation of acidic, metal-rich drainage waters; Plumlee, 1999), oxidation of other organic compounds, and volatilization of methylmercury and other volatile components. Dusts from dried, disturbed sediment deposits could expose broader populations to contaminants in the sediments.

Potential Contamination from Inundation of and Damage to Residential and Commercial Areas

There are many residential and commercial areas along low-lying portions of the coast that occur within the scenario and (or) Cal OES inundation zones (figs. 6 and 7), and that could be variably destroyed, damaged, or flooded by the tsunami. In some areas, most notably San Clemente, southern Dana Point, and Malibu Beach, only the most beachward row of residences or commercial buildings is in the scenario or Cal OES inundation zones. However, a number of residential and adjacent commercial areas are indicated to be more extensively inundated. Significant examples include Balboa Island in Newport Bay (fig. 6, completely inundated, with more than 1,300 single- and multi-family residences), other parts of Newport Bay, Venice, Oxnard, and Ventura Harbor.

Particularly in southern California, residential areas that fall within the scenario and (or) Cal OES inundation zones are dominated by high-value properties (the vast majority are from $1 million to $4 million, with some $20 million or more). Many of the residences in the inundation zones are listed in online property information databases as having been built prior to the 1970s and 1980s. If damaged by a tsunami, these older buildings could produce debris containing legacy contaminants, such as lead paint, asbestos, creosote-treated landscape timbers, mercury-bearing thermostats, and chlordane and other pesticides (Plumlee and others, 2012; Australian Broadcasting Corporation, 2013). Debris from younger buildings could include fragments of CCA-treated landscape timbers and more recently used pesticides (for example, fipronil). Debris from buildings of all ages could include fragmented electronics, plastics, mercury from fluorescent lightbulbs, fabrics and other materials containing some metal colorants (for example, hexavalent chromium), fire retardants (PBDEs), and containers of household chemicals or products, such as paints, drain cleaners, pesticides, herbicides, and fertilizers (Plumlee and others, 2012; Manuel, 2013).

For buildings that are inundated but not heavily damaged, the ground floors would likely be left with deposits of intermingled household furnishings/products, debris, containers of household chemicals, and externally derived small debris and sediments transported into the buildings by the tsunami floodwaters.

Following the tsunami, mold would likely develop in inundated houses and buildings, and debris piles (Barbeau and others, 2010; Manuel, 2013).

Figure 6. Satellite image (from appendix A *of* The SAFRR Tsunami Modeling Working Group, 2013), showing the extent of inundation of residential areas within Newport Bay.

Potential Contamination from Significant Point Sources

Analysis of the EPA facilities registry system database (U.S. Environmental Protection Agency Facilities Registry System, 2011), satellite imagery, and other GIS coverages indicates that a number of larger, environmentally significant facilities occur partially or fully within the scenario and (or) Cal OES inundation zones (fig. 3). In addition to the marine oil terminals (fig. 5), petroleum storage facilities, boat yards, and other port facilities noted in previous sections of this report, these facilities include:

- Wastewater-treatment plants;
- Non-nuclear power plants;
- Naval or coast guard facilities;
- Transportation maintenance facilities;
- Chemical manufacturing plants;
- Other types of manufacturing plants (for example, that manufacture metal products, electronics, cement, or concrete products); and
- Railroad yards, paper mills, scrap yards, big box retail stores, food-processing facilities, and several airports.

Many of these facility types may have some potential to release various types of contaminants. These include stored fuel (for example, from airports), anhydrous ammonia (for example, from refineries, chemical manufacturing plants, food-processing plants or cold food storage plants), processing chemicals (for example, acids, alkalis, solvents), manufactured chemicals (for example, borates), food products, trash, and contaminant residues from paved surfaces or soils. Some small facilities, such as dry cleaners, gasoline stations, auto dealerships, or auto body shops in the inundation zones could be localized source of contaminant releases.

Figure 7. Satellite image showing a closeup of Balboa Island, which falls completely within the scenario and California Emergency Management Agency (Cal OES) inundation zones. Of the approximately 1,300 single- and multi-family residences are on the island, many are of older construction (for example, prior to the 1970s and 1980s), and almost all are valued in excess of $1 million U.S. currency.

Wastewater Treatment Plants

Wastewater-treatment plants (WWTPs) occur partially or fully within the scenario or Cal OES inundation zones in a number of coastal cities (figs. 8 and 9), and so present a substantial potential for environmental contamination from the tsunami. These include Alameda, Arcata, Avalon, Burlingame, Cardiff, Crescent City, El Granada, Eureka, Goleta, Half Moon Bay, Hercules, Huntington Beach, Manila, Mill Valley, Morro Bay, Oakland, Oceano, Pacifica, Palo Alto, Pinole, Pismo Beach, Richmond, San Buena Ventura, San Francisco, San Leandro, San Lorenzo, San Pedro, Santa Cruz, and Tiburon. These WWTPs and their feeder sewer systems, if inundated and damaged, could release: (1) raw or partially treated sewage or other contaminated wastewater; and (2) wastewater-treatment chemicals, such as disinfectants, pH control chemicals, and oxidants. It also is possible that sewer systems outside the inundation zone that feed into damaged or shutdown WWTPs could experience backups and release raw sewage into the environment outside the inundated areas.

Many different organic and inorganic contaminants can be present in sewage and wastewater. Examples include solid fecal matter, human hormones and metabolic wastes, components of pharmaceuticals and personal care products, detergents, fire retardants, home use pesticides and rodenticides, dissolved metals, and emulsions (Plumlee and others, 2013). Pathogens that can be present include bacteria (for example, *Escherichia coli* or *Salmonella*), protozoa, enteric viruses, and parasitic worms. There also are growing concerns that some of the bacteria present in sewage and wastewater discharges may have enhanced resistance to antibiotics.

Power Plants

Non-nuclear power plants are indicated to occur partially within the scenario or Cal OES inundation zones in the following cities—Carlsbad, Eureka, Hayward, Huntington Beach, Long Beach (several), Morro Bay, Oakland, Samoa, San Francisco, and Wilmington. Based on databases available from the California Energy Commission, nearly all these power plants use natural gas or gas from municipal solid waste as their fuel. Hence, we infer that they likely do not pose a risk for the release of large volumes of environmentally detrimental chemicals or wastes.

Neither the Diablo Canyon nor the inoperative San Onofre nuclear powerplants are indicated to occur within the scenario or Cal OES maximum inundation zones. Several peripheral buildings in the San Onofre facility (which is scheduled to be retired and decommissioned) do appear to fall within the Cal OES maximum inundation zone.

Airports and Military Air Stations

Airports in several coastal cities (Eureka, Santa Barbara, Alameda/Oakland, and Oceano) and several Navy or Coast Guard air stations are indicated to fall partially or completely within the scenario or Cal OES inundation zones. There is the potential for some compromise of fuel storage tanks (where they occur in the inundation zone), damage to aircraft and aircraft maintenance/repair facilities, and runway runoff that could release some environmental pollutants, such as petroleum or tire residues.

Landfills

Landfills are indicated to occur partially or completely within the scenario or CA OES inundation zones in the following cities—Corte Madera (Marin), Huntington Beach, Long Beach (multiple), Los Angeles, Mill Valley, Newport Beach, Oakland, San Leandro, San Mateo, San Pedro, Sausalito, and Venice. In a number of cases, these are historical landfills that are currently not in use. Further investigation is needed to determine whether these landfills could be compromised sufficiently by the tsunami to cause the release of stored wastes or waste degradation products. A wide range of possible organic and inorganic chemicals can be present in landfill leachates, such as dissolved organic matter, ammonium, solvents, organohalogen compounds (PCBs, carbon tetrachloride, etc.), pesticides, phenols, plasticizers, metals or metalloids (Mn, Hg, Pb, Cr, Cd, Cu, As, Ni, etc., some organo-complexed or colloid-bound), and organic and inorganic acids. Leachates can vary as a function of the age of landfill. Damage to containment structures can cause release of gases, such as methane, hydrogen sulfide, and volatile organic compounds.

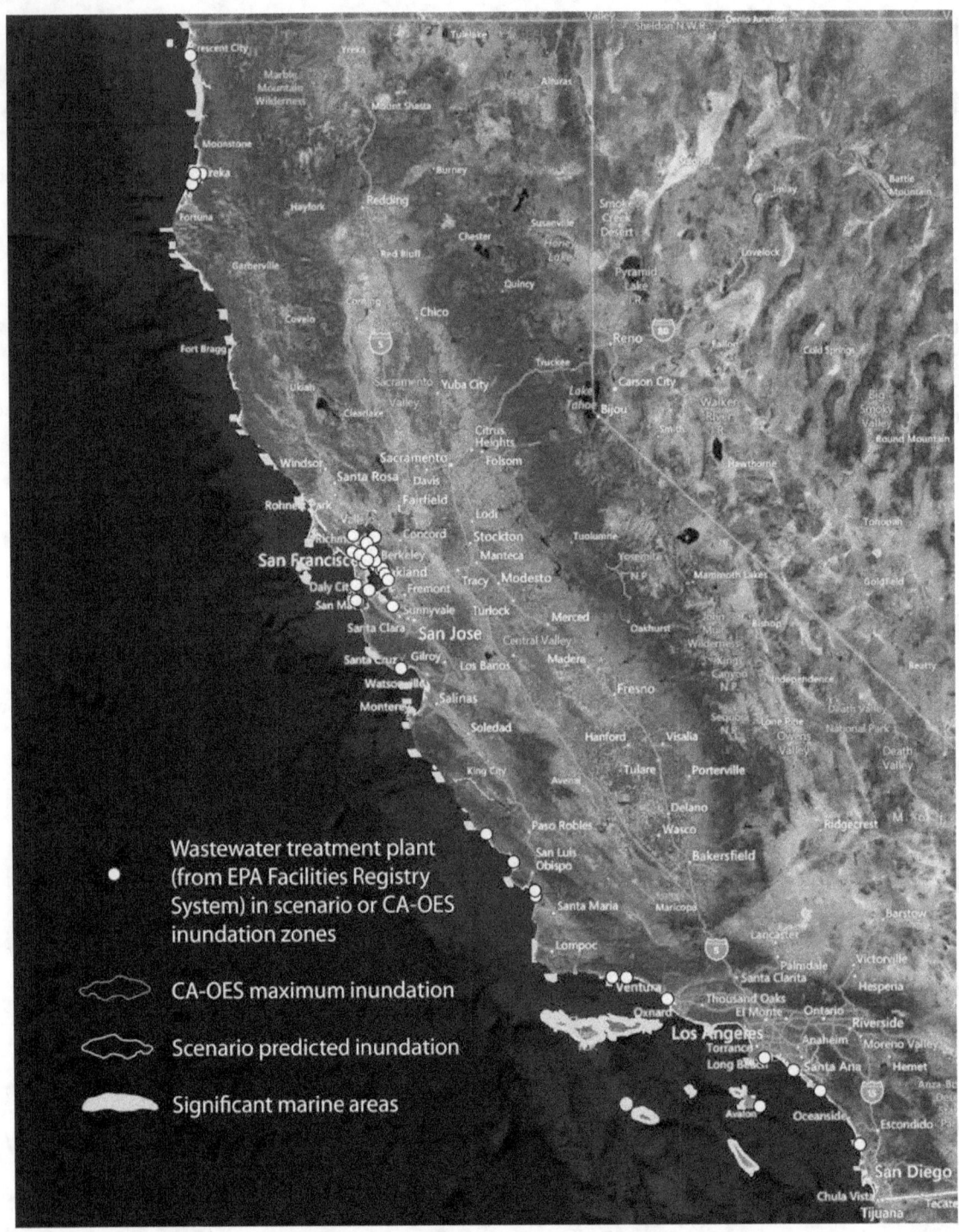

Figure 8.   Map showing locations of wastewater treatment plants (data from U.S. Environmental Protection Agency Facilities Registry System, 2011) indicated to occur partially or completely in the scenario or California Emergency Management Agency (Cal OES) inundation zones.

Figure 9. This satellite image shows a wastewater treatment plant indicated to lie partially within the scenario tsunami inundation zone (transparent blue-green). The entire area of the image lies within the California Emergency Management Agency (Cal OES) maximum inundation zone.

Potential Non-Point Source Contamination

There are various types of potential non-point sources from which contamination could be redistributed onland and into the nearshore marine environment by the tsunami. Examples include:

- Paved/unpaved surfaces and storm drains in urban, residential, and commercial areas;
- Inundated agricultural fields in coastal lowlands along river mouths;
- Wetlands and other areas that receive stormwater runoff from urban areas or major coastal highways (such as I-5 north of San Diego); and
- Large military bases with firing ranges, fuel storage areas or other coastal facilities that have not undergone environmental remediation.

Urban Areas and Highway Corridors

It is possible that tsunami flood waters could redistribute a variety of potentially hazardous surface chemicals (for example, petroleum or metal-rich residues from paved surfaces), contaminated soils, trash, storm drain sediments, and other materials from inundated urban and industrial areas and highway corridors. This would be somewhat analogous to stormwater runoff from urban areas and major highway corridors, which has long been recognized as a source of contamination with cumulative detrimental environmental effects.

Agricultural Fields

Somewhat greater areas of agricultural fields are indicated to be inundated in the northern parts of the State (for example, in the Eel River lowlands) than in the southern parts of the State. Most of these are fields in which alfalfa, hay, or other pasture grasses are grown (Ratliff, 2013). A wide range of insecticides, herbicides, and fertilizers may be applied to alfalfa and pasture grasses in California, and the types applied can vary according to many factors, such as geographic location, time of year, stage of crop growth, maturity of the field, type of insect or weed present, and nutrient status of the alfalfa (Canevari and others, 2007; Meyer and others, 2007; Summers and others, 2007; University of California Integrated Pest Management Program, 2010). Many different practices can be implemented to ensure that such chemicals are applied in ways to minimize their release into the environment by overspray, runoff, and other mechanisms. However, further investigations are needed to understand what insecticides, pesticides, and fertilizers are permitted and used in agricultural areas within the tsunami inundation zones, how they are applied, and what their potential is to be transported by the tsunami either inland or into the ocean.

Tsunamigenic Fires

As noted by Porter and others (2013) and Scawthorne (2013), oil or petroleum spills can be ignited by electrical sparks, friction, or other mechanisms. As a result, they concluded that oil-spread tsunamigenic fires would be possible in the Ports of Los Angeles, Long Beach, and Richmond, and that small, more localized fires could result at some marina fueling docks. Other flammable liquid bulk cargo, such as vegetable oil, if released, also might contribute to fires. Movement of spilled oil on water or on land would spread these fires to structures, berthed automobiles, cargo, and other port facilities. As noted by Tanaka (2012) for the Tohoku tsunami, and Porter and others (2013) for New York City port facilities flooded by Hurricane Sandy storm surge, a substantial number of fires also could be triggered by inundated vehicles, such as automobiles, forklifts, and drayage trucks at the ports, most likely due to electrical shorts. Similarly, electrical shorts in residences or commercial/industrial areas, and tsunami-downed power lines also could cause fires if electricity were not shut off prior to inundation. Analogous fires were caused by the Hurricane Sandy storm surge in New York and New Jersey—for example, 122 homes in the Breezy Point subdivision of Queens, New York, were burned as a result of a sea water-triggered electrical short at one residence (Gothamist, 2012), and other dwellings along the coast suffered fires from sparks caused by falling power lines.

Tsunamigenic fires in spilled oil, debris, cargo, vehicles, vegetation, and residential, commercial, or industrial buildings and their contents could produce potentially significant volumes of complex smoke, gases, airborne ash, residual ash, and debris. These materials could have a wide range of potential toxicants depending on the material being combusted. Potentially asphyxiant or irritant gases include carbon monoxide, hydrogen cyanide, hydrogen chloride, sulfur dioxide, hydrogen fluoride, hydrogen bromide, nitrogen oxides, and ammonia. Smoke, airborne ash, and residual ash/debris from the fires could contain, depending on the material being burned, various mixtures of (Plumlee and others, 2013): (1) caustic alkali solids; (2) lead, hexavalent chromium, arsenic, nickel, vanadium and other heavy metal(loid)s; (3) asbestos; and (4) various organic toxicants such as polycyclic aromatic hydrocarbons, formaldehyde, formalin, dioxins, and polychlorinated biphenyls.

Plausible Environmental Impacts of Damages, Debris, and Contamination

Tsunami-related damages, debris, and contamination could have a variety of short-term and long-term impacts on the environment and the health of coastal marine and terrestrial ecosystems. Details of potential ecological impacts are have been studied by D. Brosnan (written commun., 2013) of University of California, Davis.

Marine habitats in near-shore and intertidal zones along the coast and ecosystems in many coastal estuaries, marshes, sloughs, and lagoons could be damaged by physical erosion or sedimentation. These areas near inundated ports, harbors, coastal cities, and coastal agricultural areas could receive an influx of debris and contaminants. Examples of ecologically important areas near cities include the San Diego and Sweetwater Marsh National Wildlife Refuges in San Diego Bay, Seal Beach National Wildlife Refuge, Salinas River National Wildlife Refuge, Pilar Point State Marine Conservation Area/James V. Fitzgerald Marine Reserve between San Francisco and El Granada, San Francisco Bay, and Humboldt Bay National Wildlife Refuge. Some ecologically sensitive areas are fisheries for seafood such as oysters (for example, Drakes and Tomales Bays) and crabs, and so could possibly suffer damage- or contaminant-related impacts on seafood supply or quality.

Shallow aquifers in the areas of tsunami inundation could plausibly be contaminated by seawater. Transient salinization of inundated agricultural fields and salt water-triggered die offs of terrestrial vegetation in or immediately adjacent to tsunami inundation areas could also occur. Agricultural fields in the inundation zone could receive debris and sediments brought in by the tsunami.

Spilled oil and petroleum products would add to the elevated baseline of crude oil from natural seeps already present along some parts of the coast. Spilled oil and petroleum products degrade through dissolution and volatilization of more toxic components, photolytic degradation, and biodegradation. However, oil and oil-seawater emulsions could coat birds and mammals that came into contact with it, with resulting impacts on birds' flight ability and the internal heat regulation of birds and mammals. Inhalation of toxic volatile oil components, as well as dermal absorption or ingestion of oil or waters with dissolved oil components, could be toxic to marine and terrestrial organisms that contact spilled oil.

Debris and re-exposed contaminated sediments would be a source of sea- or rain-water-leachable metal and organic contaminants that could potentially pose chronic toxicity threats to marine life (for example, copper, organotin) and(or) that are bioaccumulative (for example, mercury, legacy pesticides). Atmospheric weathering of metal sulfides in exposed marine sediment deposits could generate locally acidic waters with elevated levels of potentially toxic metal(loid)s such as copper, zinc, nickel, and arsenic.

Wildlife could become entangled in debris and could ingest small debris. Ingestion, dermal absorption, or inhalation of various contaminants by aquatic, terrestrial, and avian organisms has the potential to result in short-term, acute toxicity effects, or longer-term, chronic toxicity effects.

Potential Human Health Implications

If the scenario's expected evacuation of populations from the inundation zone were to be successful, there could plausibly be few or no drownings or other tsunami-related casualties, crushing injuries, puncture wounds, or infections.

Immediately after the tsunami, human populations outside the inundation zone might be transiently exposed to airborne gases, smoke and ash from tsunamigenic fires. The intensity and duration of these exposures would be dependent on the size of the fire, weather conditions, wind direction, and other factors. Exposures to high levels of irritant gases and particulate matter in smoke could exacerbate respiratory diseases (for example, asthma, bronchitis, chronic pulmonary obstructive disease), and cause increased cardiovascular problems, such as heart attacks and strokes. The potential for longer-term health impacts from transient exposures to toxicants contained in airborne gases, smoke, and ash has not been clearly documented (or even studied) in prior fire disasters.

If widespread power outages result from the tsunami, then increased incidences of carbon monoxide poisoning from the use of portable power generators would be possible.

Infectious disease outbreaks following the tsunami would likely be prevented or mitigated by ready access of local populations to emergency relief efforts that provide clean drinking water supplies, unspoiled food, vaccinations, and other medical care.

Post-tsunami cleanup of ports, harbors, and inundated on-land areas would help reduce the potential for long-term human exposures to toxicants and pathogens in harbor waters, debris, soils, ponded waters, and buildings. Exposures to cleanup workers and people returning to inundated areas could be reduced by the use of proper personal protective equipment (such as respirators, gloves, steel-toed rubber boots, and protective clothing) and appropriate exposure mitigation practices (for example, dust control) during cleanup.

There would be some potential for increased cases of vector-borne diseases, such as mosquito-transmitted West Nile virus, but this could be mitigated by pest control measures that thwart growth of mosquito populations in ponded tsunami waters, and growth of insect and rodent populations in debris and damaged buildings. Monitoring of seafood would prevent human consumption of pathogen- or toxicant-contaminated seafood obtained from tsunami-affected areas along the coast.

Post-Tsunami Environmental Cleanup and Recovery

Debris and contamination cleanup and disposal would pose substantial logistical challenges and economic costs following the tsunami. Deposits of small debris and contaminated sediments would be a challenge to identify, access, and clean up across all affected coastal marine and estuarine environments, and so could pose a long-term source of potential contamination in sensitive ecological areas.

Based on recent past disasters, the cleanup of debris, damaged buildings, contaminated sediments, and other potentially hazardous materials in ports, harbors, and inundation areas could be expected to vary considerably in its pace from area to area—a function of economic pressures, the insurance claim process, building and cleanup regulations, the extent of damage, and other factors. Characterization of debris for the presence of asbestos, lead paint, pesticides, and other potentially hazardous materials would be required to determine if these materials would require enhanced dust mitigation and other exposure mitigation measures during cleanup, and disposal into isolated landfills.

Similarly, characterization of tsunami sediment deposits (both onshore deposits and deposits dredged to clear harbor channels) would be needed to determine whether the sediments are contaminated and therefore require more costly disposal in isolated landfills. As with the debris, the sediments would need to be characterized for contaminants such as asbestos, heavy metals, or organic toxicants. In addition, any sediments being considered for on-land disposal, particularly in areas in contact with the atmosphere or oxygenated waters should be evaluated for their acid-generating potential (see net acid production tests outlined in Plumlee and others, 2007).

Although such assessments are needed environmentally, they could add significant time to the post-disaster cleanup and recovery if not accomplished quickly. The specialized removal and disposal measures for hazardous materials also would add substantially to cleanup costs.

Actions to Enhance Resilience to Tsunamis

There are actions that can be taken by companies, individuals, and governments to help prepare for and mitigate environmental impacts of a coastal tsunami.

All businesses large and small can benefit from an analysis of their facilities' location(s) within the scenario or CA OES tsunami inundation zones, and the vulnerability of their facilities to tsunami-related or surge-related damages. Once vulnerabilities are understood, then ways to mitigate these vulnerabilities can be evaluated from a cost/benefit standpoint, recognizing the potential costs stemming from environmental liability should damage and contaminant release occur. Recognition of the impacts of coastal tsunamis and storm surges also should be accounted for in business emergency operation plans. Even small businesses can take these steps to help minimize potential impacts and liability from their own facilities, and impacts on their facilities from tsunami-related contamination.

Families or individuals that live or work in the tsunami inundation zones could benefit by developing a tsunami-related emergency plan that helps them evaluate the potential hazards, and understand how and where to evacuate prior to a looming tsunami. Steps can be taken by individuals to mitigate potential environmental impacts in and adjacent to residences in the inundation zones. These could include, for example, maintaining only minimal amounts of pesticides, fertilizers, and other household chemicals in residences, and storing potentially toxic chemicals in watertight, tethered containers. Post tsunami, it is important for residents returning to inundated homes to be aware of, prepare for, and appropriately address the potential environmental hazards that could exist. Such hazards could include, for example, mold, contaminated sediments, and toxicant-bearing debris. If present, these hazards would necessitate use of appropriate respiratory and other personal protection to prevent exposure, and likely would require specialized cleanup and proper disposal practices.

Porter and others (2013) recommend that residents and businesses in the inundation zone should be aware of flood insurance through the National Flood Insurance Program or commercial sources. An additional consideration, particularly for owners of older buildings, will be whether the flood insurance adequately covers the extra costs for removal and disposal of toxicant bearing debris.

Given the high value of the coastal residential and commercial properties in the inundation zone, it can be postulated that there would be substantial insurance claims for environmental restoration, mold mitigation, disposal of debris that contains hazardous materials, and costs of litigation related to environmental liability. These costs would likely add to the economic costs estimated by Rose and others (2013) for the scenario tsunami.

The previous section outlined the need for timely characterization of tsunami debris and sediment deposits for the potential presence of contaminants. In past tsunamis, such assessments have led to delays in cleanup and recovery (R. Wilson, Cal OES, oral comm., 2013). Development of State and local policies that plan for and facilitate rapid assessment of potential contamination, and that facilitate rapid decision making for disposal options should hazardous debris or sediment be identified, would help enhance resilience following the tsunami. Additionally, local jurisdictions with substantial residential and commercial areas within the inundation zone can utilize information in their own property databases on the age, square footage, and construction type of buildings to better plan for the amounts and types of debris that could be generated by a tsunami. Jurisdictions can work with owners of large, environmentally significant facilities (including, for example, their own wastewater treatment plants) to help assess vulnerabilities and mitigate potential damages that could otherwise lead to the release of large volumes of contaminants during a tsunami.

Summary

This study has described a number of ways by which the SAFRR scenario tsunami could produce contamination, adversely affect the nearshore marine and coastal environments, and result in human exposures to potential tsunami-generated contaminants. There are a number of uncertainties in this type of analysis. As a result, our approach and general findings should only be considered as the first of multiple steps toward a more quantitative, predictive approach to understanding the potential sources, types, environmental behavior, and environmental and health implications of contaminants that could be released into the environment by coastal tsunamis. For example, more detailed, site-specific analyses are needed of significant industrial, commercial, and residential areas that occur in the inundation zone to assess their vulnerabilities to tsunami inundation and damage, and the specific types and volumes of resulting contaminants and debris that could be released should such damage occur.

The highest potential for inundation-related damages and resulting release of significant amounts of contaminants into the inundation zone and coastal environments would likely occur in the major ports, in inundated and damaged residential and commercial areas, and from some large facilities, such as wastewater-treatment plants. A wide range of debris types and contaminants could potentially be released, depending on the source. Potential concerns include, for example:

- Complex debris;
- Crude oil, various fuel types, and other petroleum products;
- Some liquid bulk cargo and dry bulk cargo types;
- Heavy metals such as lead, arsenic, organotin, mercury, nickel, and vanadium;
- Raw sewage and chemicals used to treat wastewater;
- Organic contaminants, such as paints, legacy pesticides, current use pesticides, herbicides, and fertilizers; and
- Smoke and ash from tsunamigenic fires.

Tsunami-related physical damages, debris, and contamination could have short- and long-term impacts on the environment and the health of coastal marine and terrestrial ecosystems. If human populations are successfully evacuated prior to the tsunami arrival, there would be no or limited numbers of drownings, other casualties, or related injuries, wounds, and infections. Immediately after the tsunami, human populations outside the inundation zone could be transiently exposed to airborne gases, smoke, and ash from tsunamigenic fires.

Post-tsunami cleanup, if done with appropriate mitigation (for example, dust control), personal protection, and disposal measures, would help reduce the potential for cleanup-worker and resident exposures to toxicants and pathogens in harbor waters, debris, soils, ponded waters, and buildings. A number of other steps can be taken by governments, businesses, and residents to help reduce the environmental impacts of tsunami and to recover more quickly from these environmental impacts.

References Cited

Australian Broadcasting Corporation, 2013, Tsunami leaves Japan with toxic asbestos legacy: Australian Broadcasting Corporation, Lateline transcript, accessed August 28, 2013, at http://www.abc.net.au/lateline/content/2013/s3678154.htm, Jan 28, 2013.

Barbeau, D.N., Grimsley, L.F., White, L.E., El-Dahr, J.M., and Lichtveld, M., 2010, Mold exposure and health effects following hurricanes Katrina and Rita: Annual Reviews in Public Health, v. 31, p. 165–178.

Barberopoulou, A., Borrero, J.C., Uslu, B., Kalligeris, N., Goltz, J.D., Wilson, R.I., and Synolakis, C.E., 2009, Unprecedented coverage of the Californian coast promises improved tsunami response: Eos, Transactions of the American Geophysical Union, 90(16), pp. 137–138.

Basnayake, B.F.A., Chiemchaisri, C., and Mowjood, M.I.M, 2005, Solid wastes arise from the Asian tsunami disaster and their rehabilitation activities—Case study of affected coastal belts in Sri Lanka and Thailand, in Proceedings Sardinia 2005: Cagliari, Italy, Tenth International Waste Management and Landfill Symposium, 7 p., accessed August 28, 2013, at http://www.swlf.ait.ac.th/data/pdfs/715`.pdf.

Bird, W.A., and Grossman, E., 2011, Chemical aftermath-contamination and cleanup following the Tohoku earthquake and tsunami: Environmental Health Perspectives, v. 119, p. A290–A301.

Canaveri, M., Vargas, R.V., and Orloff, S.B., 2007, Weed management in alfalfa, Chapter 8, in Irrigated Alfalfa Management: Berkeley, University of California Agriculture and Natural Resources Publication 8294, 19 p., accessed August 28, 2013, at http://alfalfa.ucdavis.edu/IrrigatedAlfalfa/pdfs/UCAlfalfa8294Weeds_free.pdf.

Cedre, 2004, Vegetable oil spills at sea—Operational guide: Centre of Documentation, Research and Experimentation on Accidental Water Pollution, 36 p., accessed August 28, 2013, at http://www.cedre.fr/en/publication/operational-guide/vegetable-oil/vegetable-oil.php

Cedre, 2013, Spills: Centre of Documentation, Research and Experimentation on Accidental Water Pollution, accessed August 28, 2013, at http://www.cedre.fr/en/spill/alphabetical-classification.php.

Chagué-Goff, C., Niedzielski, P., Wong, H.K.Y., Szczuciński, W., Sugawara, D., and Goff, J., 2012, Environmental impact assessment of the 2011 Tohoku-oki tsunami on the Sendai plain: Sedimentary Geology, v. 282, p. 175–187, doi:10.1016/j.sedgeo.2012.06.002.

Gothamist, 2012, Photos—Surreal devastation of Breezy Point after Hurricane Sandy: accessed August 28, 2013, at http://gothamist.com/2012/10/31/photos_the_devastation_of_breezy_po.php#photo-1.

Johnson, A., Golding, S., and Coots, R., 2006, Chemical characterization of stormwater runoff from three Puget Sound boatyards: Washington State Department of Ecology Publication 06-03-041, 57 p., accessed August 28, 2013, at https://fortress.wa.gov/ecy/publications/summarypages/0603041.html.

Keim, M.E., 2011, The public health impact of tsunami disasters: American Journal of Disaster Medicine, v. 6, p. 341–349.

Lynett, P., and Son, S., 2013, Port and harbor hydrodynamics, *in* Geist, E.L., ed., Modeling for the SAFRR tsunami scenario—Generation, propagation, inundation, and currents in ports and harbors: U.S. Geological Survey Open-File Report 2013–1170–D, p. 106–119.

Manuel, J., 2013, The long road to recovery—Environmental health impacts of hurricane Sandy: Environmental Health Perspectives, v. 121, p. A152–A159.

Meyer, R.D., Marcum, D.B., Orloff, S.B., and Schmierer, J.L., 2007, Alfalfa fertilization strategies, Chapter 6, *in* Irrigated alfalfa management: Berkeley, University of California Agriculture and Natural Resources Publication 8294, 16 p., accessed August 28, 2013, at http://alfalfa.ucdavis.edu/IrrigatedAlfalfa/pdfs/UCAlfalfa8292Fertilization_free.pdf.

National Oceanic and Atmospheric Administration, 2013, National Geophysical Data Center Tsunami Event web site: National Oceanic and Atmospheric Administration, August 28, 2013, at http://earthquake.usgs.gov/earthquakes/eqinthenews/2004/us2004slav/#summary.

National Oceanic and Atmospheric Administration Fisheries Service, 2013, Impacts of oil on marine mammals and sea turtles: National Oceanic and Atmospheric Administration, accessed August 28, 2013, at http://www.nmfs.noaa.gov/pr/pdfs/health/oil_impacts.pdf.

Plumlee, G.S., 1999, The environmental geology of mineral deposits, *in* Plumlee, G.S., and Logsdon, M.J., (eds.), The environmental geochemistry of mineral deposits, Part A. Processes, Techniques, and Health Issues: Society of Economic Geologists, Reviews in Economic Geology, v. 6A, p. 71–116.

Plumlee, G.S., Foreman, W.T., Griffin, D.W., Lovelace, J.K., Meeker, G.P., and Demas, C.R., 2007, Characterization of flood sediments from hurricane Katrina and Rita and potential implications for human health and the environment, *in* Farris, G.S., Smith, G.J., Crane, M.P., Demas, C.R., Robbins, L.L., and Lavoie, D.L., eds., Science and the storms—The USGS response to the hurricanes of 2005: U.S. Geological Survey Circular 1306, p. 246–257.

Plumlee, G.S., Morman, S.A., and Cook, A., 2012, Environmental and medical geochemistry in urban disaster response and preparedness: Elements Magazine, v. 8, p. 451–457.

Plumlee, G.S., Morman, S.A., Meeker, G.P., Hoefen, T.M., Hageman, P.L., and Wolf, R.E., 2013 (in press), The environmental and medical geochemistry of potentially hazardous materials produced by disasters, *in* Lollar, B.S.L., ed., Treatise on Geochemistry, Second Edition, Volume 9: Amsterdam, Netherlands, Elsevier Science, 648 p.

Porter, K., Byers, W., Dykstra, D., Lim, A., Lynett, P., Ratliff, J., Scawthorn, C., Wein, A., and Wilson, R., 2013, The SAFRR Tsunami Scenario—Physical damage in California: U.S. Geological Survey Open-File Report 2013-1170–E, 183 p.

Ratliff, J., 2013, Agricultural damages from the SAFRR tsunami scenario, in Porter, Keith Byers, W., Dykstra, D., Lim, Amy, Lynett, P., Ratliff, J., Scawthorn, C., Wein, A., and Wilson, R., The SAFRR Tsunami Scenario—Physical Damage in California : U.S. Geological Survey Open-File Report 2013-1170–E, p. 127-139.

Ratnapradipa, D., Conder, J., Ruffing, A., White, V., 2012, The 2011 Japanese earthquake—An overview of environmental health impacts: Journal of Environmental Health, v. 74, p. 42–50.

Wein, A., Rose, A., Wing, I.S., Wei, D., and 2013, Economic impacts of the SAFRR tsunami scenario in California: U.S. Geological Survey Open-File Report 2013–1170–H, 46 p.

Scawthorn, C., 2013, Fire following tsunami—A contribution to the SAFRR tsunami Scenario: SPA Risk LLC, accessed August 28, 2013, at http://www.sparisk.com/pubs/Scawthorn-2013-SAFRR-FFT.pdf.

Sekizawa, A., and Sasaki, K., 2011, Overview of fires following the great East-Japan earthquake: Fire Science and Technology, v. 30, p. 91-100.

Shibata, T., Solo-Gabriele, H., and Hata, T., 2012, Disaster waste characteristics and radiation distribution as a result of the Great East Japan Earthquake: Environmental Science & Technology, v. 46, p. 3,618–3,624.

Srinivas, H., and Nakagawa, Y., 2008, Environmental implications for disaster preparedness—Lessons learnt from the Indian Ocean tsunami: Journal of Environmental Management, v. 89, p. 4–13.

Stratus, 2006a, Treated wood in aquatic environments—Technical review and use recommendations: Stratus Consulting, prepared for National Oceanic and Atmospheric Administration, National Marine Fisheries Service, accessed August 28, 2013, at http://swr.nmfs.noaa.gov/wood/copperwood_report-final.pdf.

Stratus, 2006b, Creosote-treated wood in aquatic environments—Technical review and use recommendations: Stratus Consulting, prepared for National Oceanic and Atmospheric Administration Fisheries, accessed August 28, 2013, at http://swr.nmfs.noaa.gov/wood/creosote_report-final.pdf.

Summers, C.G., Godfrey, L.D., and Natwick, E.T., 2007, Managing insects in alfalfa, Chapter 9, *in* Irrigated alfalfa management: University of California Agriculture and Natural Resources Publication 8295, 24 p., accessed August 28, 2013, at http://alfalfa.ucdavis.edu/IrrigatedAlfalfa/pdfs/UCAlfalfa8295Insects_free.pdf.

Tanabe, S., and Subramanian, A., 2011, Editorial—Great eastern Japan earthquake—Possible marine environmental contamination by toxic pollutants: Marine Pollution Bulletin, v. 62, p. 883–884.

Tanaka, T., 2012, Characteristics and problems of fires following the great east Japan earthquake in March 2011: Fire Safety Journal, v. 54, p. 197–202.

Tioga, 2002, Seaport plan waterborne cargo forecast update: Prepared for the San Francisco Bay Conservation and Development Commission by the Tioga Group, 27 p.

University of California Integrated Pest Management Program, 2010, Pest Management guidelines—Alfalfa: University of California Integrated Pest Management Program, Publication 3430, 94 p.

United Nations Environment Programme, 2007, After the tsunami, coastal ecosystem restoration—Lessons learnt: United Nations Environment Programme, accessed August 28, 2013, at http://postconflict.unep.ch/publications/dmb_tsunami_coastal.pdf.

U.S. Environmental Protection Agency Facilities Registry System, 2011, U.S. Environmental Protection Agency facilities registry system: Environmental Protection Agency Facilities State Single File CSV Download, downloaded May, 2011, from http://www.epa.gov/enviro/html/frs_demo/geospatial_data/geo_data_state_single.html.

U.S. Geological Survey, 2013, Magnitude 9.1—Off the west coast of Sumatra: U.S. Geological Survey web site, accessed May 2013 at http://earthquake.usgs.gov/earthquakes/eqinthenews/2004/us2004slav/#summary.

U.S. Geological Survey Seeps, 2013, Natural oil and gas seeps in California: U.S. Geological Survey web site, accessed June 2013 at http://walrus.wr.usgs.gov/seeps/index.html.

Van Geen, A., and Luoma, S.N., 1999, The impact of human activities on sediments of San Francisco Bay, California—An overview: Marine Chemistry, v. 64, p. 1–6.

Water Resources Action Plan, 2009, Final 2009 water resources action plan: Ports of Los Angeles and Long Beach report, accessed August 28, 2013, at http://www.portoflosangeles.org/environment/wrap.asp.

Weston, 2009a, Summary of sediment quality conditions in the port of Long Beach: Weston Solutions Report prepared for Port of Long Beach, accessed August 28, 2013, at http://www.portoflosangeles.org/DOC/WRAP_POLB_Sediment_Quality_Summary.pdf.

Weston, 2009b, Summary of sediment quality conditions in the port of Los Angeles: Weston Solutions Report prepared for Port of Los Angeles, accessed August 28, 2013, at http://www.portoflosangeles.org/DOC/WRAP_Appendix_B1.pdf.

Wilson, R.I., Admire, A.R., Borrero, J.C., Dengler, L.A., Legg, M.R., Lynett, P., McCrink, T.P., Miller, K.M., Ritchie, A., Sterling, K., and Whitmore, P.M., 2013a, Observations and impacts from the 2012 Chilean and 2011 Japanese tsunamis in California (USA): Pure and Applied Geophysics, v. 170, p. 1,127–1,147.

Wilson, R., Davenport, C., and Jaffe, B., 2012, Sediment scour and deposition within harbors in California (USA), caused by the March 11, 2011 Tohoku-oki tsunami: Sedimentary Geology, v. 282, p. 228–240.

Wilson, R.I., Barberopoulou, A., Miller, K.M., Goltz, J.D., and Synolakis, C.E., 2008, New maximum tsunami inundation maps for use by local emergency planners in the State of California, USA: EOS Trans. American Geophysical Union 89(53), Fall Meeting Supplement, Abstract OS43D-1343.

Yamada, T., Hiroi, U., and Sakamoto, N., 2011, Aspects of fire occurrences caused by tsunami: Fire Science and Technology, v. 30, n. 4 (special issue), p. 101–105.

Yoshii, T., Imamura, M., Matsuyama, M., Koshimura, S., Matsuoka, M., Mas, E., and Jimenez, C., 2012, Salinity in soils and tsunami deposits in areas affected by the 2010 Chile and 2011 Japan tsunamis: Pure and Applied Geophysics, 20 p., doi:10.1007/s00024-012-0530-4.